No More FEAR

Steps to Permanently Removing Fear from Your Life

Sigma S. Smith

For No More FEAR: Steps to Permanently Removing Fear from Your Life

Bulk Ordering Information:

Special discounts are available on quantity purchases by churches or other religious organizations. For details, contact the publisher.

Bookstores and wholesalers should contact the publisher for purchasing information.

God hath not given us the spirit of fear; but of power, and of love, and of a sound mind. (2 Timothy 1:7 KJV)

Table of Contents

DEDICATION

This book is dedicated to my brother Omara. He was one of my biggest cheerleaders, and he will always live in my heart.

ACKNOWLEDGEMENTS

I want to thank my mom and dad (Apostle Kenneth and Pastor Fodie Smith) for being awesome pastors and parents.

I want to thank, my sister, Marisa for helping me stay on task.

I want to thank my brother KT and my nieces Ariyanna and Kiera for their support.

I also want to thank the countless people who have supported and encouraged me throughout this process.

I love you all!

INTRODUCTION

God wants you to live in abundance, but in order for abundance to manifest in your life, you must be obedient when He asks you to do something. Unfortunately, many of us fail to act because of fear. Fear has handcuffed me for years and has prevented me from walking in my true purpose and living my best life. It caused me to become complacent and accept my situation even though I was miserable. I finally decided that if I wanted to receive everything God has for me, I had to exercise my faith and stop allowing fear to hinder my destiny. This book is one of the results. I encourage you to follow the steps outlined in this book. If you want to truly experience God's best, you must rid your life of fear.

CHAPTER 1: WHAT IS FEAR?

2 Timothy 1:7 says that God did not give you the spirit of fear but of power, love and a sound mind (2 Timothy 1:7). James 1:17 says every good and perfect gift comes from above (James 1:17). Since fear does not come from God, it is not beneficial to you, and you should want to eliminate anything from your life that is not from God.

When I was meditating on the word fear, God gave me a definition based on the acronym FEAR. FEAR stands for the **F**AILURE to **E**NTER into **A**BSOLUTE **R**EST™ regarding anything God instructed you to do. In other words, fear is when you allow people, circumstances and negative thoughts to prevent you from being obedient to God's mandate on your life. The mandate could be a book God told you to write 10 years ago or a business that He told you to start, or an idea that He told you to implement.

In Genesis 22, God told Abraham to offer his son, Isaac, as a burnt offering. Abraham did not hesitate. He was obedient to God, and the next morning he and Isaac travelled to the place where God instructed them to go. As they prepared to build the altar, Isaac asked Abraham about the lamb that they were going to use as a sacrifice. Abraham's response was that God would provide a lamb. Abraham built the altar, bound Isaac, and placed him on the altar. As Abraham raised his knife to kill Isaac, an angel from heaven spoke. He told Abraham not to kill Isaac because Abraham had proven his faith in God by his willingness to sacrifice his only son. When Abraham looked up, he saw a ram trapped in the bushes. He used the ram as the sacrifice. God then told Abraham that because of his willingness to give up his son, He was going to multiply his seed and his possessions. Had Abraham operated in fear and not absolutely rested in the instruction that God gave him, he would not have received the blessing from God.

The takeaway from Abraham's story is that when God tells you to do something, you have to be obedient to His voice and immediately take action. You must not allow fear to rob you of your blessing. Be confident that when God tells you to do something, He already knows that the outcome will be favorable! Through the prophet Isaiah in Isaiah 41:10, He says to fear not because He is with you, and to be not dismayed because He is God. He said that He would strengthen you. He said that He would help you. He said He would uphold you with the right hand of His righteousness. You have a better covenant than Isaiah because God lives in you! He has already walked out every step for you, so He knows EVERY single difficulty that you are going to face. He already knows that you will be victorious, so you have to ABSOLUTELY REST in everything He says!

The good news is that if you have missed it, if you have allowed fear to hinder your purpose, you still have time to get it right. God loves you unconditionally, and He does not hold your past against you. I know because I have missed it. God has given me so many ideas over the years, but I never implemented any of them because of fear. I allowed the devil to take advantage of my insecurities, by flooding my mind with doubt and fear, believing that my ideas were not good and that my business ventures would not succeed. I was too busy focusing on negative thoughts that I failed to remember that the word of God said that I could do all things through Christ which strengthens me. I finally decided that I would no longer allow fear to prevent me from receiving the things that God has for me.

CHAPTER 2: THE RELATIONSHIP BETWEEN FEAR AND LOVE

As you just read, God did not give you the spirit of fear. Since fear does not originate from God, love does not exist where there is fear, because God is love (1 John 4:16). This is further validated by 1 John 4:18 which says that there is no fear in love because perfect love casts out fear (1 John 4:18). Have you ever been in love? I have. The guy that I loved could do no wrong in my eyes. I completely trusted him, and believed everything he said. This is an example of perfect or mature love, and perfect love casts out fear because it allows you to absolutely rest in what the person you love says to you. The problem with having perfect or mature love for people is that sometimes the love is not reciprocated.

In my case, the man that I loved eventually gave me reasons not to trust him, and when that happened my perfect or mature love for him was ruined. When your love for God is perfect or mature, you completely trust Him, and you will do anything He asks of you. The beauty of having perfect love for God is that His love is always reciprocated. God loved you before you even existed, and He will never give you a reason to doubt His love for you.

The second part of 1 John 4:18 says that fear has torment (1 John 4:18). One definition of torment is worry (Dictionary.com). Fear has torment, or fear worries because it **F**ails to **E**nter into **A**bsolute **R**est™ concerning the promises of God. David's love for God allowed him to suppress fear and doubt, and boldly confront

Goliath, despite Goliath's massive size. While his brothers and other members of the army were fearful of Goliath, David was unafraid. He courageously fought and killed the giant with only a slingshot and rocks. David was able to fulfill his God-ordained purpose because he absolutely rested in the belief that God would give him the strength to defeat Goliath.

CHAPTER 3: REASONS TO LET GO OF FEAR

There are many negative effects of fear, but there are four reasons you need to immediately remove it from your life. The first reason is that when you walk in fear you CANNOT please God. Hebrews 11:6 says "but without faith it is impossible to please Him: for he that cometh to God must believe that He is, and that He is a rewarder of them that diligently seek Him" (Hebrews 11:6). According to Hebrews 11:1 faith is believing in what you cannot see. Since faith is the opposite of fear, fear is believing in the truth of your current challenging situation instead of absolutely resting in what God told you. When you are not faithful to what God says, you cannot please Him!!

In Mark 4, Jesus and the disciples were on a boat when it began to storm. The winds and waves were so high that water began to flood the ship. Jesus was asleep in the back of the ship. He was absolutely resting, but the disciples grew afraid and woke Him. When Jesus woke up, He was not afraid. He immediately rebuked the wind and spoke to the sea, and the storm ceased. Jesus, who was not happy about being awakened from His sleep, asked His disciples why were they afraid and where was their faith. The disciples did not understand that God's protection was all around them, and all they had to do was follow Jesus' example and rest. Their failure to rest was displeasing not only to Jesus, but also to the Father.

The second reason you need to remove fear now is that when you operate in fear you cannot completely trust God. In Matthew 14, Jesus was walking on water. Peter was in the ship and said to Jesus if that is really You, let me walk onto the water with You. Jesus told him to come and Peter actually started walking on the water. A sudden wind arose and Peter grew fearful and began to sink. As long as Peter absolutely rested in Jesus' words and trusted Him enough to come out into the sea, he was able to perform the seemingly impossible task of walking on water. As soon as he started to operate in fear and abandon his faith in the word of God, he began to fail. Proverbs 3:5 & 6 says to trust in the Lord with all of your heart and lean not to your own understanding. In all of your ways acknowledge Him, and He will direct you. If you want God to direct every aspect of your life, you must let go of fear and completely trust Him.

The third reason why you need to remove fear now is when you operate in fear you cannot receive God's best. In Matthew 19, a wealthy young man asks Jesus what he could do to receive eternal life. When Jesus gave him the list of commandments, his response to Jesus was that he had kept all of the commandments. He again asked Jesus what he needed to do. Jesus told him to sell all of his possessions and give the proceeds to the poor. The young man walked away disappointed because he was afraid to part with his possessions. The young man did not have faith that God would have returned all his wealth, plus more, if he had absolutely rested in Jesus' instructions and gave away all of his possessions. Many of you are in the same position as the young man. You are satisfied with living a comfortable life, a life that you and many others consider "good." You do not understand that if you completely rely on God's Word, and rest in EVERYTHING He tells you to do, you can live your BEST life.

The fourth and final reason why you need to remove fear now is because fear keeps you from walking in your God-ordained purpose. When you operate in fear you are reluctant to do what God has called you to do. The reluctance is born of the fear of failure and self-doubt. Understand that when God calls you, He qualifies you. When He tells you to do something, He has already equipped you to complete the task. 2 Corinthians 12:9 says "my grace is sufficient for you, for my power is made perfect in weakness" (2 Corinthians 12:9). The only thing you have to do is obey His voice. God knows that you cannot handle the task alone. His power within you is what allows you to be successful.

God called Moses to lead the children of Israel out of Egypt. Despite all of the miracles that God allowed Moses to witness, Moses was afraid that he did not have the ability to lead. Exodus

4:10 tells us that Moses told God that he did not feel he was qualified because he had a speech impediment. God reassured Moses that he was capable. Moses lead the children of Israel for a season, but it was ultimately his inability to trust God, or rest in what God told him to do, that prevented him from leading them into the Promised Land.

How many times has God told you to do something, but you made excuse after excuse as to why you could not do it? As I stated earlier, God has given me so many ideas over the years. One of the ideas was a book, but because of fear I never made an effort to get it published. I am an attorney with an English degree, but I did not feel that I was qualified to write a book. I did not think anyone would be interested in reading what I had to say. When one of my family members or church family members asked me about the book, my response was I will finish it in a couple of months. Guess what? Month after month passed and I never made an effort to complete it. Now, I understand that my fear to publish the book delayed my destiny and paralyzed my purpose. I would be so much further today had I immediately walked in obedience to God's calling on my life. You do not have to make the same mistake that I made. I admonish you to learn from my missteps, and let go of your fear and step into God's purpose for your life today.

CHAPTER 4: STEPS TO OVERCOMING FEAR

Faith is the opposite of fear. Therefore, the key to overcoming your fear is exercising your faith. Romans 10:17 tells us that faith comes by hearing the word of God, so when you are removing fear from your life, it is extremely important that you read and meditate upon the word of God daily. When negative thoughts of fear and doubt enter your mind, you can easily replace them with the word of God. There are three steps to exercising your faith. You must speak. You must believe. You must Act.

Step 1 – Speak

The first step is speaking. You must say the right things. You must call those things that be not as though they were, or confess what you want to see (Romans 4:17). Mark 11:23 says that you will have what you say. Affirm the Word of God by confessing the promises of His word.

Affirmations are an essential part of my daily fellowship with God. Making affirmations was one of the things that helped me get through the bar exam. Although I had always done well academically, I started to experience feelings of self-doubt about my ability to pass the exam. I heard stories from many different sources that people like me, who did not attend law school in North Carolina, had a really difficult time passing the North Carolina bar exam. Instead of giving into fear, I affirmed my faith in God's purpose for my life. The more and more I made affirmations, the easier it was to for me to rid my mind of negative thoughts and visualize myself passing the exam. Guess what? I passed it the first time.

Speak: Make the following confessions at least once daily. Remember faith comes by hearing, and hearing by the word of God (Romans 10:17).

Affirmation 1

Father, I declare that I am free from fear because You did not give me the spirit of fear but of power, love and a sound mind. Therefore, no matter what challenges I face, I will enter into ABSOLUTE REST regarding the thing that You have instructed me to do.

Affirmation 2

Father, I declare today that You are my light and my salvation, so I will not operate in fear. You are the strength of my life, so I will not be afraid. I am operating in perfect love, therefore fear cannot exist in me.

Affirmation 3

Father, I declare right now that Fear cannot exist in my life. I will not believe what I see, but I will believe what You told me about my situation. I am trusting in You with all my heart and I'm leaning not unto my own understanding. In all my ways I acknowledge You, and You are directing my path. You are leading me into my greatness! I will no longer settle for a good life because I am ready to receive Your best!

Step 2 - Believe

The second step in exercising your faith is believing. Speaking the right words is important, but your words are useless if you do not believe what you are saying. Mark 11:23 also says that when you speak you cannot doubt, but must believe that what you say will happen. Believing is related to your mind. When the negative thoughts of fear and failure invade your mind, you have to cast them down according to 2 Corinthians 10:5 and spend time meditating on what the word of God says about your situation. Another way to reign in your thoughts is by visualizing yourself doing what God asked you to do.

During my first year of law school, I had to take a closed book exam. The test was 4 hours, and my grade on the exam was going to determine my grade for the entire course. Even though I was prepared, when it was time for me to take the exam I was very anxious. So, I went into class that day, picked up an exam and took my seat. When I opened the exam, my mind went completely blank. Negative thoughts of fear and failure began to flood my mind, and I was afraid. I got up from my seat and went to the rest room. I began to cast down those thoughts of fear and doubt by envisioning myself passing the exam. When I returned to my seat, I looked at the questions again, and the information came back to me. I was able to regain my composure because I believed that I had the knowledge and ability to pass the exam.

Believe: Spend at least 20 minutes daily (10 minutes in the morning and 10 at night) meditating on what God told you to do. Visualize yourself doing what He asked you to do. One key to believing is seeing it in your mind. When negative thoughts try to invade your mind, cast them down and read and meditate on the following scriptures:

I can do all things through Christ which strengtheneth me. (Philippians 4:13)

Now unto him that is able to do exceeding abundantly above all that we ask or think, according to the power that worketh in us. (Ephesians 3:20)

Ye are of God, little children, and have overcome them: because greater is He that is in you, than he that is in the world. (1 John 4:4)

But thanks be to God, which giveth us the victory through our Lord Jesus Christ. Therefore, my beloved brethren, be ye stedfast, unmoveable, always abounding in the work of the Lord, forasmuch as ye know that your labour is not in vain in the Lord. (2 Corinthians 15:57 & 58)

And let us not be weary in well doing: for in due

season we shall reap, if we faint not. (Galatians 6:9)

For verily I say unto you, That whosoever shall say unto this mountain, Be thou removed, and be thou cast into the sea; and shall not doubt in his heart, but shall believe that those things which he saith shall come to pass; he shall have whatsoever he saith. (Mark 11:23)

This book of the law shall not depart out of thy mouth; but thou shalt meditate therein day and night, that thou mayest observe to do according to all that is written therein: for then thou shalt make thy way prosperous, and then thou shalt have good success. (Joshua 1:8)

And this is the confidence that we have in him, that, if we ask anything according to his will, he heareth us: And we know that he hear us, whatsoever we ask, we know that we have the petitions that we desired of him. (1 John 5:14 & 15)

What shall we then say to these things? If God be for us, who can be against us? (Romans 8:31)

For I know the thoughts that I think toward you, saith the Lord, thoughts of peace, and not of evil, to give you an expected end. (Jeremiah 29:11)

Step - 3 Act

The third and final step in exercising your faith is action or doing whatever God told you to do. You will never see the manifestation of God's word in your life, if you do not take action. Faith without works is dead (James 2:20). This scripture means that your actions are an indication to God that you believe what He said. God is faithful, and when you absolutely rest in the things that He told you to do, you are able to take action without hesitation!

When I was in high school, I was interested in going to a summer program that had locations all over the country. When I saw the different locations, I immediately knew that I wanted to go to Los Angeles. I had never been to California, and I really wanted to see the Hollywood sign. God had already told me I would be accepted into the program in Los Angeles. But, in order for me to get in, I had to apply. All of the affirming and believing would have been useless had I not applied to get into the program. I applied, got in, and ended up in Los Angeles!

Act: Think about one thing that God told you to do but you have not done because of fear. Now decide today to be obedient to His calling on your life. Figure out what it is going to take to accomplish it. If you do not know how, ask God! If you ask Him for direction, He will give it to you or send someone across your path to assist you.

Remember, God is omniscient! He knows all, so all you have to do is tap into His unlimited knowledge.

CONCLUSION

Fear is not going to leave you overnight. It is a process. The key to conquering anything is consistency! When I was learning how to drive a manual shift car, I had to practice driving everyday until I was able to shift gears without causing the car to jerk back and forth. Practicing consistently allowed me to become proficient in driving. The same is true for overcoming fear. If you are consistent in following these steps, you will see results. Your faith will become so strong that fear will not stand a chance because fear cannot exist in the presence of faith!

ADDITIONAL FEAR MEDITATION SCRIPTURES

Yea, though I walk through the valley of the shadow of death, I will fear no evil: for thou are with me; thy rod and thy staff they comfort me. (Psalm 23:4)

The Lord is my light and my salvation; whom shall I fear? The Lord is the strength of my life; of whom shall I be afraid? (Psalm 27:1)

The Lord is on my side; I will not fear: what can man do unto me? (Psalm 118:6)

Be strong and of a good courage, fear not, nor be afraid of them: for the Lord thy God, he it is that doth go with thee; he will not fail thee, nor forsake thee. (Deuteronomy 31:6)

And David said to Solomon his son, Be strong and of good courage, and do it: fear not, nor be dismayed: for the Lord God, even my God, will be with thee, until thou hast finished all the work for the service of the house of the Lord. (1 Chronicles 28:20)

For I the Lord thy God will hold thy right hand, saying unto thee, Fear not; I will help thee. (Isaiah 41:13)

BONUS AFFIRMATION

Father God in the name of Jesus, I declare and decree that this is the day that You have made, and I will rejoice and be glad in it. Today is going to be a great day! Nothing is going to happen that You and I cannot handle! I thank You for ordering my steps today. I thank You for granting me favor on today. I will allow my light to shine so that people will see my good work and glorify You. No weapon formed against me will prosper and EVERYTHING that I do will prosper!

ABOUT THE AUTHOR

Sigma S. Smith was born and raised in Fayetteville, North Carolina. She is an Author, Professional and Personal Development Strategist, Attorney, Public Speaker and Minister. Her mission is to empower women to discover their God-ordained purpose, pursue their passion and embrace their greatness.

She obtained her undergraduate degree from Duke University and her law degree from Catholic University, Columbus School of Law and is a member of the North Carolina State Bar. She was called into the ministry in August 2002. Since that time, she has served as a youth minister at Evangel Temple Christian Center.

To contact Sigma for workshops, speaking and hosting opportunities please email her at: graced4greatness@gmail.com.

www.ingramcontent.com/pod-product-compliance
Lightning Source LLC
Chambersburg PA
CBHW071449040426

42445CB00012BA/1503